Global Warming

by Ellen Lawrence

Consultants:

Daniel Shepardson
Departments of Curriculum and Instruction and Earth, Atmospheric, and Planetary Science
Purdue College of Education, West Lafayette, Indiana

Kimberly Brenneman, PhD
National Institute for Early Education Research, Rutgers University
New Brunswick, New Jersey

New York, New York

Credits

Cover, © Triff/Shutterstock, © Smileus/Shutterstock, © Vladimir Melnik/Shutterstock, and © egd/Shutterstock; 2–3, © Jan Martin Will/Shutterstock; 4, © Urbanlight/Shutterstock; 5TL, © Photobank Gallery/Shutterstock; 5CL, © Istock/Thinkstock; 5BL, © Istock/Thinkstock; 5R, © Pavel L Photo and Video/Shutterstock; 8, © Vasilyev Alexandr/Shutterstock; 8–9, © Mike Theiss/Corbis; 10, © ssuaphotos/Shutterstock; 10–11, © egd/Shutterstock; 12, © Istock/Thinkstock; 13T, © Yuriy Kulik/Shutterstock; 13, © Glenn R Specht-grs photo/Shutterstock; 14, © Cosmographics; 15, © Kevin Schafer/Minden Pictures/FLPA; 15T, © Robert St-Coeur/Shutterstock; 16, © Olena Mykhaylova/Shutterstock; 17L, © Lloyd Thornton/Shutterstock; 17R, © Igor Grochev/Shutterstock; 18, © miker/Shutterstock; 19, © Viappy/Shutterstock; 20, © Monkey Business Images/Shutterstock; 21L, © Shutterstock; 21TR, © Tom Wang/Shutterstock; 21BR, © BestPhotoStudio/Shutterstock; 22, © Pressmaster/Shutterstock; 22R, © Olga Popova/Shutterstock; 23TL, © kilukilu/Shutterstock; 23BL, © Goodluz/Shutterstock; 23TR, © Tom Wang/Shutterstock; 23BR, © Gencho Petkov.

Publisher: Kenn Goin
Creative Director: Spencer Brinker
Design: Emma Randall
Photo Researcher: Ruby Tuesday Books Ltd

Library of Congress Cataloging-in-Publication Data

Lawrence, Ellen, 1967– author.
  Global warming / by Ellen Lawrence.
     pages cm. — (Green world, clean world)
  Audience: 5–8.
  Includes bibliographical references and index.
  ISBN 978-1-62724-104-5 (library binding) — ISBN 1-62724-104-3 (library binding)
  1. Global warming—Juvenile literature. I. Title.
  QC981.8.G56L39 2014
  363.738'74—dc23
                              2013041867

For more information, write to Bearport Publishing Company, Inc., 45 West 21st Street, Suite 3B, New York, New York 10010. Printed in the United States of America.

10 9 8 7 6 5 4 3 2 1

Contents

A Big Problem

Each day, people use a huge amount of **energy**.

Energy is the power that comes from electricity, **coal**, oil, and other **sources**.

Every time you switch on a light or ride in a car, you use energy.

Making and using lots of energy, however, has created many problems for our planet.

One of the biggest is **global warming**.

Fuels that make cars run, such as gasoline, are sources of energy. Natural gas is another type of energy. It's used to power stoves and heat homes.

How many ways have you used electricity today? In a notebook, write them down.

What Is Global Warming?

Earth is surrounded by **gases** called the atmosphere.

Some of these gases, such as carbon dioxide and methane, are called **greenhouse gases**.

Greenhouse gases trap some of Earth's heat, which is good.

Plants and animals need heat to live.

If people add greenhouse gases into the atmosphere, however, too much heat gets trapped.

Then Earth gets too warm, causing global warming.

How Do Greenhouse Gases Trap Heat?

sun

Light from the sun creates heat on Earth that plants and animals need to survive.

- Greenhouse gases got their name because they act like a greenhouse, a building that traps the sun's heat so that the plants inside can stay warm and grow.
- Greenhouse gases trap the sun's heat in the atmosphere, just like a greenhouse.

light

Some of the heat on Earth escapes back into space.

heat

Some of the heat is trapped on Earth by greenhouse gases in the atmosphere.

atmosphere

Earth

Electricity

One way people cause global warming is by making electricity.

Electricity is a type of energy that is made in factories called power plants.

To make electricity, many power plants burn coal.

Unfortunately, burning coal releases harmful amounts of greenhouse gases into the atmosphere.

coal

gases

Some power plants burn natural gas to make electricity. Just like coal, when natural gas is burned, it releases carbon dioxide and other greenhouse gases into the air.

a coal-burning power plant

9

More Harmful Gases

harmful gases

People also cause global warming when they drive cars, trucks, and other vehicles.

Fuels made from oil power most of these vehicles.

When fuel is burned in a vehicle's engine, greenhouse gases are released.

Every minute a car's engine is running, it is producing harmful gases. For one week, keep track of how many trips you take in a car. In a notebook, record the number of trips and how long each one lasts.

Oil, coal, and natural gas are known as **fossil fuels**. That's because they are made from the remains of plants and animals that died millions of years ago.

Why Is Global Warming a Problem?

Global warming is causing many places on Earth to get hotter.

As a result, some streams, rivers, and lakes could dry up.

If that happens, people and animals might not have enough water to drink.

In cold, icy places, such as the North Pole, warmer temperatures are melting the ice.

Less ice could mean disaster for some animals that live in these cold places.

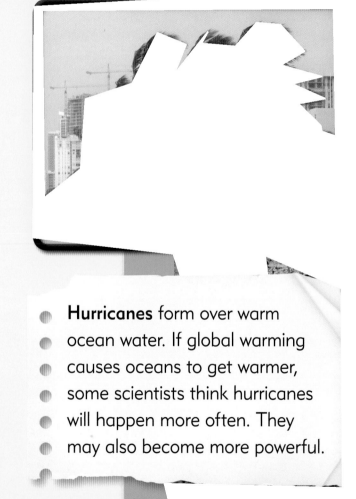

Hurricanes form over warm ocean water. If global warming causes oceans to get warmer, some scientists think hurricanes will happen more often. They may also become more powerful.

Global warming could turn this lake into dry ground.

Melting Homes

The North Pole and the area around it is a huge mass of ice that floats on the sea.

Polar bears live on the ice and hunt seals that swim in the sea.

Because Earth is getting warmer, the ice is melting.

Polar bears need the floating ice, however, to get close enough to seals to catch them.

If the ice melts, many polar bears might not get enough food and could die.

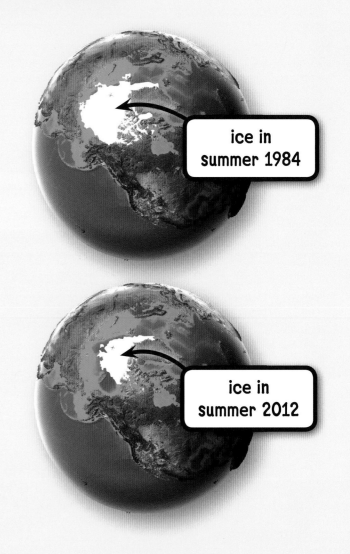

ice in summer 1984

ice in summer 2012

Seals are the main food of polar bears. The bears wait for seals by holes in the ice. They catch them when the seals stick their heads out of the water to breathe.

seal

melting ice

polar bear

Slowing Down Global Warming

Global warming can be harmful, but there are ways to slow it down.

People can burn less coal and natural gas to make electricity.

This will cut down on the amount of greenhouse gases that people release.

Instead of burning fuel, electricity can be made using the sun, wind, and water.

Making electricity in this way produces little or no harmful gases!

Solar Power

solar panels

Energy from the sun is called **solar energy**. Solar panels capture sunlight and use it to make electricity.

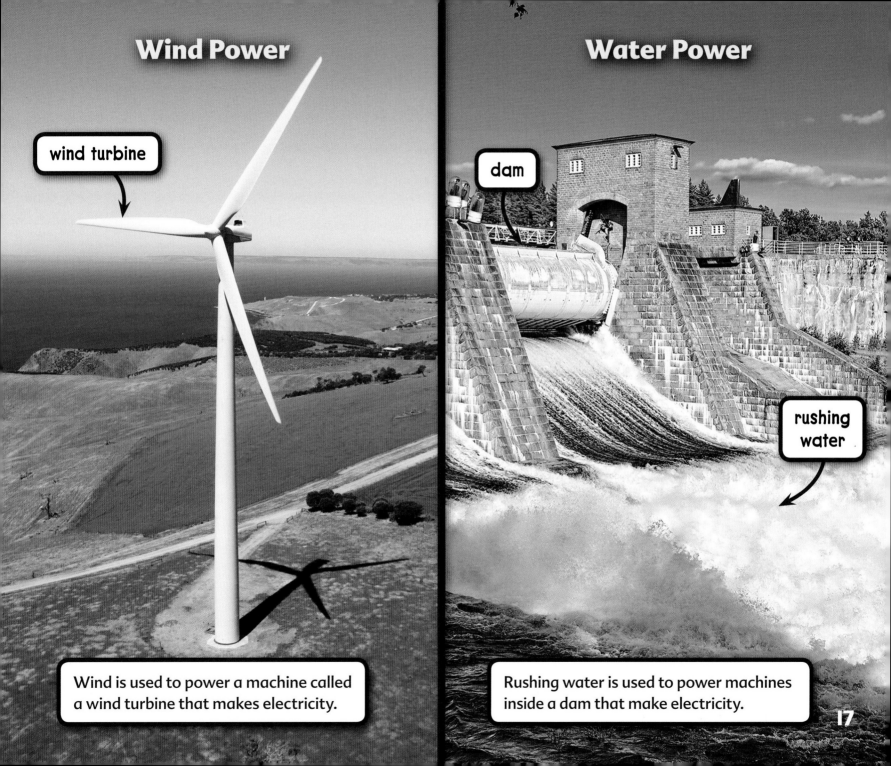

Wind Power

wind turbine

Wind is used to power a machine called a wind turbine that makes electricity.

Water Power

dam

rushing water

Rushing water is used to power machines inside a dam that make electricity.

17

Saving Energy

Every day, people take billions of trips in vehicles.

Using less gas and taking fewer trips will also help slow down global warming.

Many cars use about five gallons (19 liters) of fuel to travel just 100 miles (161 km).

Some energy-saving cars, however, use only half that amount of fuel.

They also release only half the amount of harmful greenhouse gases!

Traveling by bus instead of by car can help slow down global warming. Why do you think this is?
(The answer is on page 24.)

electric car

Some cars run on electricity instead of gas. As a result, they release fewer greenhouse gases.

Electric cars are recharged at the end of long trips.

Everyone Can Help!

Global warming is a big problem, but it's not too late to help solve it.

Making electricity without burning fossil fuels will release fewer harmful gases.

Using less electricity and taking fewer car trips will help, too.

Everyone can do something to help solve the problem, so let's get started today!

It's best to buy appliances with an Energy Star label. A dishwasher with this label uses less electricity than one without the label.

Be an Energy Saver!

Ask your parents to turn off the engine if the car is waiting at the curb and not moving.

In winter, shut doors quickly when you enter or leave your home. Otherwise, lots of heat will escape, which wastes energy.

If it's safe, try walking or biking instead of riding in a car.

Science Lab

Find out how good you are at saving energy by recording on a chart all the energy-saving things you do each week.

Be an Energy Saver

Begin by thinking about all the ways you can save energy.

Make a section for each of your ideas on a chart.

Every time you save energy, give yourself a check mark.

At the end of the week, count the marks to see how many times you were an energy saver.

Then see if you can do better the next week!

My Energy-Saving Chart

	Week 1	Week 2	Week3
Switched off a light	✔ ✔ ✔		
Reminded an adult to switch off a light	✔		
Unplugged my computer	✔ ✔		
Walked to school instead of riding in a car	✔		

Science Words

coal (KOHL) a black, rock-like type of fossil fuel that is dug from the ground and can be burned to make electricity

energy (EN-ur-jee) power, such as electricity, that machines and vehicles need in order to work

fossil fuels (FOSS-uhl FYOO-uhls) fuels, such as coal, oil, and natural gas, that formed deep underground from the remains of plants and animals that died millions of years ago

gases (GASS-iz) matter that floats in air and is neither a liquid nor a solid; most gases, such as carbon dioxide, are invisible

global warming (GLOHB-uhl WARM-ing) the heating up of Earth's air and oceans caused by gases that trap the sun's heat in Earth's atmosphere

greenhouse gases (GREEN-*houss* GASS-iz) gases, such as carbon dioxide and methane, that collect in Earth's atmosphere and trap heat

hurricanes (HUR-uh-*kanes*) violent storms with very strong, swirling winds

solar energy (SOH-lur EN-ur-jee) energy that is created by light from the sun

sources (SORSS-iz) the things from which other things come

Index

Read More

Metz, Lorijo. *What Can We Do About Global Warming? (Protecting Our Planet).* New York: Rosen (2010).

Spilsbury, Louise. *The Environment (Investigate).* Chicago: Heinemann (2009).

Learn More Online

To learn more about global warming, visit

www.bearportpublishing.com/GreenWorldCleanWorld

About the Author

Ellen Lawrence lives in the United Kingdom. Her favorite books to write are those about nature and animals. In fact, the first book Ellen bought for herself, when she was six years old, was the story of a gorilla named Patty Cake that was born in New York's Central Park Zoo.

Answer for Page 18

A bus can carry about 50 people at once. If all those people traveled in cars, many more vehicles would be releasing harmful gases.